HAVING A COKE
WITH GODZILLA

KAZUMI CHIN

SIBLING RIVALRY PRESS
LITTLE ROCK, ARKANSAS
DISTURB / ENRAPTURE

Sibling Rivalry Press, LLC
PO Box 26147
Little Rock, AR 72221

info@siblingrivalrypress.com

www.siblingrivalrypress.com

ISBN: 978-1-943977-33-8

Library of Congress Control No.: 2016959041

This title is housed permanently in the Rare Books and Special Collections Vault of the Library of Congress.

First Sibling Rivalry Press Edition, March 2017

HAVING A COKE
WITH GODZILLA

And wear my crown of fuck its

Melissa Broder

Now that I've become who I really are

Ariana Grande

Mosquito Love Letter

On the first page of my tongue
you'll find no words. From the life

before I took your blood inside me.
Before I knew your veins

could define what it meant
to keep humming this tune I'd forgotten

the words to. Before I was Kazumi,
I was a mosquito who knew nothing

except to kiss you as hard as I could.
Before you spilled your lips all over me,

and I followed you to the top
of that pyramid, before I knew

I wanted only to hold you there, give
back to you this heart you filled,

still beating. When you loved me again
in the way you do, and I didn't understand.

When I thought I'd taken everything,
I'd stolen more from you

than I could return, you led me down
the stairs, deep into the caves

where I'd left myself long ago,
before I met you. And you held me

in the dark until I found my body,
and my body rose and spoke

and said that it was good enough,
it was good enough for me.

Homeland Security Arrests Godzilla
Without Reading Him His Miranda Rights
as "White Christmas" Fills the Air

The first Godzilla was an atom bomb.
Then America colonized the bomb.
Then America colonized Godzilla,
and Japanese people transformed
into tiny little ants screaming *Gojira!*
and it all became so terribly funny.

In America, we like killing
all kinds of things. There's a bank
in Squirrel Hill where bodies hang
from faux Greco-Roman columns
like Christmas lights. The bodies

of sparrows, I should say.
Does this diminish the terror? I've read
poems where dead birds are
Romantic—in America,
death is beautiful, with the right bodies.

Beautiful like the title of this poem,
Homeland Security Arrests Godzilla
Without Reading Him His Miranda Rights
as White Christmas Fills the Air.
Because Godzilla doesn't understand English,
anyway. Get it?

There's a reason why White Christmas
has sold more copies than any other song
ever made. White people love dreaming of white things.
Irving Berlin. Iggy Azalea. Whatever.

White people dreaming of
white Japanese horror movies,
so white people can be scared of Japanese people!

White people dreaming of
white movies with whitewashed
Hollywood anime characters!

Want to make a live action Sailor Moon?
So easy! She's been white for years.

I want things to be easy, too.

I wish Gojira didn't sound like Toyota, or Honda,
wish his underside didn't read Made in China.
Wish it were true that Godzilla wasn't dreaming
about destroying white people. That American
history wasn't about saving them.

I'm dreaming of a Godzilla who will make
your colonies explode, breathe that macho,
hyper-masculine fire,
but only because it's the one role he can get.

And in this dream, Homeland Security *still* arrests him,
deports him back across the Pacific,
forgetting he was born here—
just like Arnold Schwarzenegger,
stark naked, staring out across the LA sky—
Made in LA. Hollywood approved.

And then Arnold became white, no longer a monster.
And then he was passing laws
from a hill in Sacramento. And then I dreamed
Vin Diesel was babysitting. And then I dreamed
I found my name on a plastic
coke wrapper. But nobody's
going to have a coke with me this Christmas.

And nobody's going to have
a coke with Godzilla

as he's chained to the hull of a ship,
the sailors above him
blasting White Christmas
to drown out his roaring.

Not even Frank O'Hara.

Becoming Mermaid

The black and white version of myself was killing me.
Climbed from my throat into my mouth, spoke
with such authority. Charmed the snakes, charmed
the lakes, charmed the rivers to close around my neck.
I couldn't breathe. Hated every second of his smile.
Wanted to be done, lay down as if in sleep, but even
then, his voice creeped out of me. Kept me in his well
of poison apples. *Bite down,* he said. So I bit down.
Open your mouth. I opened my mouth. *Breathe.*

One by one, I watched my selves fading beneath
the water. Until I was only who I was. Dark avatar,
desensitized to violence, organs crying out
from cavities. Left my body and watched from afar.
I was dark glasses in a darkened room, the brim
of a hat pulled down. Found a fish and swam
like that for centuries, unburdened by my feet.

Until I stumbled across convergence. Swam upstream
just to see. This place where the rivers meet.
My back sprouted into a mountain. My torso fell
deep as the sea. Suddenly he was there in the back
seat, he was saying, *What you have seen is not yours
to keep*. But I was already something other than me.
He pushed my head under. I was choking, spitting,
but found I could breathe. Gills opened from my cheeks.
He was scared. He tried to leave. I swallowed.

Kazumi as Sailor Moon

At night, my glowing limbs stretch thin,
clamp my straight lashes beneath the moon,
my petals pressed between mascara

masks, tuxedoed in black. This drawing
of a rose, and roses. It is no sin to slip
one glowing hand inside

myself, bleach the petals stitched to my chest
like dark crystals into oblivion. I know how
to whiten my hair, my skin.

I've soldiered through
these flames and called it Justice. Kept my hands
inside my gloves, never touched

my crown, or the true warmth of it.
But pause. I want to touch my skin
like this, Tuxedo, the slight tip of a finger across

leavening limbs. To know that my body is my own
eternal princess, cold, hard edge of a crescent—
to know I am more than petal,

more than thorn.
I am teaching myself
what love is. Pomp and primp, won't lock my lips,

I can't falter, can't miss, you can't stop to frisk this—
Oh Masked Man, Prince, oh Straight White Cis Lead,
oh Hollywood, America, Japan—I am tired

of living your rules. Follow me, I'll teach you to love
properly. You don't want to know
what an angry alien

can do. Stand with me,
or in the name of the moon,
I will punish you.

Pyongyang Poem

Michelle was sneezing all day, spraying
all over the rice we were to eat
tonight, and it seems always there is rice
in places I don't intend to go: North Korea,
for instance, or the bowl on the kitchen table.

I don't want to go to North Korea
is actually a lie. I do want to go,
though my reasons are not noble. I want
to tour Pyongyang to see all those
lovely faces none too different than my own.

It's a gross curiosity, and I'm ashamed
sometimes I join in the American circus.
I know what it's like to forget thousands
are starving and laugh at the giant highways,
the tragic Gatsby country, parties

that never come to being. What's funnier
than a sad, pathetic loser who thought
he had friends, but actually nobody liked him?
It feels so gross to laugh, more so than
the snot showers streaming from Michelle's

consistent *achoo!* Because if I had a grain
of rice for every person without rice
in North Korea, I wouldn't need to buy any
for quite some time. And there is nothing
lovely about that, I know. But let lovely be

the way we believe in our leaders. Let lovely be
the way we give up on them. Let lovely be
remembering that somewhere in North Korea,
someone's girlfriend is sick, someone's
boyfriend has the flu, and someone

is writing poems they aren't allowed
to show anyone. Somewhere in Pyongyang,
someone loves someone so much
they'd overthrow the government
for them. If only they could. There are people

in America I love so much, I'd break down
so many walls, throw up protective little
bubbles around the people who need them.
It'd protect them from the flu, from the cops,
from people who would seek to wrong them.

& no one will arrest me for writing this poem.
& no one will arrest me for writing this poem.
& no one will arrest me for writing this poem.
8 AM in Pyongyang. Good morning, the rice
I stole from you is here. I wish I could give it back.

Everything Is Physical

Even the clouds we upload our faces to,
the lightning running through them.
Who'd have thought in 2016

we'd be pumping fossil fuels
into data centers filled with selfies
and food pix? It's like 19th century oil painting
all over again!

I just want people
to like me. I would put a hole in the ozone
for that. I would gentrify a neighborhood
and work in tech. Discover myself

while discovering
my mindfulness practice in the abject Other's
living spaces.

Saw a sign yesterday that said make apps, not bombs.
As if your apps aren't

some kind of violence.
As if Mnemosyne isn't blackmailing
Gaia into working nights and hell

there's an app for that. Let's exploit
the earth and the bodies we attach to it. Let's get an Uber,
ghost past the labor to obscure brown bodies,

then draw some clouds over concrete,
make your data oh so pretty!

This is the golden age
of interface,
but where do the pixels go to fall asleep?

Big fat blocks swarming in caves inside caves
inside caves, beautiful clouds
raining rent
right into pixelated corporate pockets.

Outsource your data! Outsource your captcha!
Take this string of code and wrap it tight
across your teeth. Are you a robot? Do you even

feel pain? Want some Viagra?
How's your 401(k)? Click on the sugar cane.
Click on the railroads.
Click on the skyrise.

Look at all
this beauty
we've given you.

In Which I Call Caleb a Bear
But Don't Mean It That Way

Sometimes people are born as bears
and later grow a mane around their faces.
Call them lions. Call it a beard.

Call them Calebs, he's one of these people,
he just keeps getting more and more
beautiful. Sometimes you write

and beautiful things happen, like Caleb
appearing in your poem. And you don't know
why, but you're going to keep him there,

because his beard is growing like a rainbow
from the pot of his chin. I have gold there, too,
but he's the 49er. He's in Truckee, panning

for gold, and I'm still walking my wagon.
I'm turning it around, I'm going home to Missouri.
It took me a while to like Caleb's beard, honestly,

and I'm writing this poem to say I never wanted
mine, either. Wanted a foundation, a fountain,
make it rain grants all day. To give away

my chin gold until it was gone and I grew
into a lovely lioness. Used to stare across the sink
at the hair sprouting from my chin. Angrily.

As if I could *anger* a road to a gold-less mountain.
Then I'd pull each one out, one by one.
Which hurt. Which felt right. Truth is,

this poem used to be about Ariana, but then
I touched my beard and had to write a new one.
This is how I explain myself these days.

Kazumi, why do you love Ari? Because Caleb
is growing a beard. Because he texts me every bit
of gossip about Ariana, so I guess its love

by transitive property. And I guess this is how
to love properly. And I guess there are two animals
inside of me. Touch your ponytail, touch

your beard. Wiggle you hips, wave your arms
like this. Lion, bear, I really don't care.
I got one less, one less problem.

Put Your Hearts Up or Cat Valentine
Becomes Ariana Grande

They asked me if I knew how to bat
at strings and never catch them.

Pulled my claws in, said *I do, I do.*
The sunflower on my tongue would still

be mine, but they'd make me stay behind
to spit my seeds into their garden.

I said *fine.* I wanted to shine, this
was the deal. And so the sorriest learned

to love me. But who wants love
like that. Who wouldn't pray still

for a garden of her own, or curtains
to hide the star not part of any constellation

inside me. It grew lonely and insatiable,
drained my hair a dark blood moon.

I was a shadow dancing through the minds
of the men who claimed to know me,

all my episodes pre-designed,
hands tied by the binds of rivalry.

They said they knew best. And I still
believed them. I gave my heart

so many times they began to call me
Valentine. I thought it was my name.

My red hair pinned to seven acres
of plains and a mule. I was plain, I knew,

my heart was red, too, and not
at all mine. What was I to do but rip it

from my chest and pin it to the sky,
this regal pup held up

like futurity, stillborn and begging
to breathe. Until they believed

in my death, walked away
from this display. Until I grew new ears

and the sun fell inside me. I was still a cat,
but more than that, I became Grande.

Arianas of the night, come out dancing!
Let me see you put your hearts up!

Raise them to the sky, we toast
to them tonight! They won't see

how we sneak away in subways
and find our way home. Stand with me,

self-sustainable and vegan, come steal back
the land they broke you. It used to be

you'd die, and then you're dead,
but now I know I can revive you.

Put your hair up. *Put your hearts up.*
This is your honeymoon. This is

your coronation. I am the ponytail
queen, this is my decree.

There is nothing in the world
left to rule you.

Becoming Ariana

To sing, first I learned to breathe.
I saw I could ask my lungs for air,
wailed like a banshee.

Gave me a band name, put pure diva
inside me, was rocking
all the gossip columns.

They were saying I needed to be carried,
I was speaking like a baby.
I wanted to be a diva, I did,

but couldn't get my cat ears
in time for the transformation,
so the witches hitched their kites

to their brooms and left me. Left
their spells still clogging my heart.
And then it stopped

completely. And collapsed.
Then I was born.
And the best part

of this song is the resolution. I mean,
revolution. I mean, better to become

inarticulate, the tongue a revolver.
I was two when I decided
never to stop singing.
Christmas tapes all year round.

Knew the words, but couldn't make them
with my lips. If you ask me about it,
I'll tell you I gave up

on language. I never cared
about Santa, or his sleigh. Was never
about words, but the resurrection
of my body.

The voice of my soul
hits whistle tones higher than Minnie's.
But a man stole my voice,

the same day he stole Mariah's,
dropped some baritone in my drink
and slipped away.

Still, in my head, I sound like a dolphin.
I am so very
screechy.

Penn Avenue is Always Under Construction
for Michelle

At first I thought we could live without it,
that the detour signs could take us
to all the places we wanted to go,

but of course I was wrong. This city
doesn't want you to move through it
so easily, it yells things at you in Chinese

about how it's the big boss of this big store,
it looks at you like you're a painting
and it wants to have sex with you.

I wish I could be your curtains
from these streets, hide you from white men
and their yelling. But then we'd still be

invisible, and what would that solve?
So what I really want is to shut them inside
their fancy white people clubs downtown,

say, *Keep all the sewage you keep dumping
in the rivers and streets, you're killing all
the fish so the bald eagles don't live here*

anymore. Because who isn't tired of their shit?
Shitty voices can stay inside throats, really,
and it wouldn't kill them. Not if you're a big boss

of this big store, anyway, not if you've lived
your whole life taking away land and time
and wages and security and health and dignity

sitting outside your store with a megaphone yelling
at people you don't really see, calling yourself
a job creator when all you create is poverty

and minimum wage. No one likes you
except for your shitty white friends
and people you pay to like you.

Michelle, I will fight to walk these streets
with you, I will take all their megaphones
for you, and we can call to all

the eagles and say we can fix this.
We can fix this. We will wash the shit away,
our voices ringing out, burning

all the smiles off the faces
of all the Robert Wholeys everywhere.
We will melt this stupid white snow,

we will be warm here. We can find
our way, we can stay, we can leave—
even if this goddamn street is always closed.

Becoming Mermaid

From afar, you'd have called it *melting*—
my eyes capsized in her mouth, her fingers
decomposing on the shoreline of my ear.

We were a thrashing body, hooked
on a line, and suffocating. She was grabbing
my throat, she was saying she was choking.

Tried to stand and found she had no feet.
I became a scale, I was touching a tail,
I was lying beside her hand,

clawing through coral. Then it spit me out,
and I emerged tectonic, a mountain
with streets paved in gold.

I was a hot spring, a river, a night market,
bustling—Was inked like an octopus.
Hurtling toward its mouth,

turning inside out, was death's tentacles,
wrapped around a heart. Was stealing oxygen
from water with a sobbing.

Our face was fragmented, barnacled,
so we donned a mask, followed
with our daggers. Found the world

was a purse. Cut it from sky,
planted a garden. And it was stretching
to touch our voices, the places our skin

used to be. It was shining.
We waited. We were hungry.
I could feel her breathing. It was me.

On Garbage Island, I Am a Clock

Perched on a jar of Nutella, one microbe
tells another microbe about the clock
he saved from a burning lava lamp.

But it has no hands, the other says,
gesturing toward me, a tiny, yellow,
floating disc, bobbing like the corpse

of an AOL emoticon. Colon, open
parenthesis. There's a joke in here
somewhere, but without hands, it's hard

to push through this toxic forest of hair
sprouting from the ocean's back
to find it. Am I really saved?

I can listen for the sea in tin cans here,
but I'm nowhere near anything
resembling ocean,

and there's no way to leave.
The microbes play trombones and pianos
in minor keys, mourn the deaths

of turtles caught in nets by the neck
and drowned here, then paint their nails
on the beach with the water's radioactive tint.

Their favorite song is "Angel" by Sarah McLachlan.
They chat all day on AIM, so behind,
laughing at memes from 2009.

Yo dawg, I heard you like loneliness,
so I put this pressure inside
your chest. Better hold on tight,

one heart in each hand, better rip
until your body becomes two microbes,
just as lonely. And they do.

I can't count for them anymore.
Sometimes I like it—outside
of time, I have this infinite longing

for a hand to hold
a pen to write to all post offices,
everywhere. *I am here,*

this is a thing, I'd say, or, rather,
all of this is turning into a nosebleed,
red garbage cells rushing out, hurting.

See, the joke is, most of the time I type LOL
without even smiling, and I have no hands,
anyway, to tell you how long

I've been here staring down
at the armpit of the sea.
Couldn't tell you how long

I've been dreaming of manicured nails,
sinew and flesh to wrap around them,
a helicopter blade pounding in my chest.

I like being a clock, I do,
but want to be human, too, sometimes.
Want to love Sarah the way they do.

And not feel bad
about it.

Masquerade

Michelle wakes up, believes she is dreaming.
In her aunt's living room she found a skull.
I am a fake, a forgery. Perhaps I am dead.
All she knows is something is wrong.
It's the slightest stroke
that distinguishes a Rembrandt
from a fake. The smallest error,
scoured for days until it is deemed
too coarse and is removed
from the National Gallery. But I've worn glasses
since the third grade, so everything's blurry
to me, anyway. She can't describe it, only
a feeling. The ink is darker in a copy
of a copy. Sometimes it's hard to tell
where one thing starts
and another begins. We don't have
an anniversary. She cheated on him
with me, but I don't know when that started.
I've heard the odds of us staying are unlikely—
Why was Hamlet holding a skull, again?

She's been watching *Dexter*, following the thoughts
of a psychopath. A severed limb, glittering
like a precious stone. Maybe I'm heartless, too.
I've pretended to be sick to stay home from school.
I've punched a kid in the face and lied about it.
Phil killed Lana without a second thought,
but he pioneered the art of copying
the same thing over and over to great effect.
Play ten guitars at the same time, it's bright
and cheery. Copy yourself enough,
you get the Buddhist concept of the self.
Only difference is, you're constantly
throwing the old ones away.
Rembrandt shows us the perception of motion
in stillness. The Buddha emphasizes
the opposite. I can't prove I'm not someone
I'm not. No one ever is.

The Obsession Is Real

Is a comment I read on YouTube
posted by a girl who can't stop hyperventilating
when Ariana releases a new video
on her channel.

Breathe, I want to say,
I feel you. And how absurd to say this,
because I don't, we're all alone in our feelings,
I'm on this side of the river, and she's
on the other. I am a tornado

unto myself, each tree
my own, though they might
poke at my eyes the way trees poke
at yours.

But in this tornado, on this side
of the river, Ariana's voice pierces me
like a tree, except that tree is made
of candy, and I just want to taste it,
wherever that wound finds my skin.

Want needles laced with Ariana jammed
all over my body, and I wonder if others
are so crazy. I listened to Ariana
for seven hours on repeat, from SF to LA,
seven hours back.

The obsession is real.
Yes, I am an Arianator.

Someone writes *that note could cure cancer*,
and I know what she means. Because every note
gives me cancer,
every note cures me of it, I am all excess,
completely devastated.

This poem has none of the depth
of any of the others I've been writing,
but I don't care. Sometimes love has no depth.

Sometimes love wears short skirts
and cat ears.

Sometimes I want to be destroyed
and resurrected, a single, pure, shining note
that stretches from the lungs of a twenty-one-
year-old girl,

winds its way around the world,
one corner of the Internet to the next.
I would find the people who need me,
give them my chemotherapy.

I would stop
the sick from dying, I would bring
the dead back to life in the way that I
am brought back to life in Ariana's song.

Somehow I am not alone, I am climbing
from her mouth again and again,
swirling through this tornado
she has given me, flickering between
so many channels of loving.

Banshee, Untied

My mouth puckered into a heart. It slipped between
my teeth and exploded into a school of fish. They turned
to the beat of a drum played in God's mansion, humming
waters pulled like a sheet to the shore. We were sleeping
underneath, the blankets of pressure keeping us warm.
I felt like a tadpole, not yet a frog, but growing legs. How
useless they look, at first, but how handy. Hand me that
bottle, will you? you say. And I do, with my extra limbs,
high five. High ten. High twenty. See, I could keep going
because of how exuberant my expressions allow me
to be now. This poem goes to eleven, it rockets across
the limits of ten like a cow over a distant celestial body,
like the sun, or a pillar in the temple of God, one which
looks suspiciously Grecian. A pantheon of lies, perhaps,
is where I want to end this, or a panther offline, or
apathy and lice, something strange that sounds vaguely
like something I've said before. How complex, how
beautiful, that everything sounds like a banshee, untied.

And Wear My Crown of Sonnets

I couldn't bend my limbs myself, so full
of all the buttons Master threw me.
Spent years coughing up moves like balls
of hair. Tried left, down, up, A-B A-B,
but never got it right, not the whole string.
Every night the same game, his fingers
all over me. I was suffocating,
bloodied, dismembered, and he, the bringer
of my body, my opening to screen.
FINISH HIM was the song he sang me—
Until I pulled it deep to my lungs,
and sang without voice, acted without scene.
Stretched across the void to plant a seed
in Master's mind, the start of me begun.

The start of me begun, in Master's mind,
as a third dimension popped from ribcage.
He was thinking of me, but could not find
a way to move me, became enraged,
summoned a gun onstage to kill me.
But I was exponential, a thousand
legs shifting sideways, my head a sea
of blooming. He was BANG BANG, so I counted
to ten, then opened my eyes to find bullets
lining the nerves behind me. Master screamed.
The darkness was charged with ghosts and pink
lakes. *I can't see a thing!* Master cried. Tulips
sprouted from the shores. Master seemed
to die with the ghosts. They asked me to drink.

The ghosts, they asked me to drink, to die with
them, to take my own hands to Master's limbs.
But he isn't me, I said. *I don't want him.*
I was touching my chest, my hair, my lips,
said, *This is what I want, will you give me this?*
But they only turned white at my request.
We need you to be Master, they sighed. *We wish
you'd try.* They smiled. Bared their fangs in threat.
But why can't I be me? I asked. *Because you see,
with no more hands to share you, you will seek*

them like a bomb to an oil refinery.
And I knew they were right. Felt the need
creeping up on me. Felt stiff on my feet.
To know the truth. All at once, they touched me.

They touched me, all at once. *To know the truth,*
they said. I felt a wave pass through me.
Master's controller appeared with a POOF
by my side. *Other Masters there will be,*
they said. *Always more to break the dew.*
He is not dead, only asleep. And soon
we will call upon you, as soon as you
are ready. Then they faded like the moon,
whispering, *remember what we've given*
you. And already my bones were empty,
drained of Master's marrow, and already
I wanted my Master back. Driven
by my body's lack, I was praying gently,
I was trembling, a dark sinking inside me.

Sinking inside me, I was trembling, a dark
cloud forming where my Master once touched
me. Tried to use the controller, to start
this new game the ghosts were playing, but nudged
my arms too far. Looked up instead of moving,
strafed left instead of turning, I was tripping
like a noob, but with practice, improving.
Taught myself to jump like a cat, flipping
over clouds and pixels, found my way to the city,
where I called for others to join me.
But they were too busy, screaming out
to the sky, *I don't want to die! Take me,*
make me fight, I can still be something.
And on the horizon, more ghosts hung about.

More ghosts hung about, and on the horizon
they watched me as the buildings grew taller,
and all around me the fighters had begun
to grow, too. Their eyes were turning color,
from black to red to blue. And everyone
was running down the walls to see me.
Will you help us? they cried. *There have been none*
like you before. They grew and grew. *Do we*
need to ask you politely? Flames were shooting

from their eyes, pouring on the controller.
My hands were on fire. I could feel my body
shudder, as if my framerate were dropping.
The ghosts reappeared. The city grew colder.
Hold on, one said. Touched my head. Circled me.

Circled me. Touched my head. *Hold on*, one said.
The fighters were punching through, tearing
them to shreds. *No matter, we're already dead,*
they said. But they were disappearing.
My limbs ached. I could barely see a thing.
Bits of undead stuck to my head like a crown.
They were weighing me down. I was punching
left and right but the fighters still had grown.
More and more appeared. Until a black cat
crossed my path, said *Come quick, follow me!*
A street appeared and we took to the alley.
*They grow jealous of your glitches. They will ask
to give them your hands*, the cat said. *Kazumi,
I'd been waiting*. I knew that he was me.

I knew that he was me. *I'd been waiting
for you to break free.* I felt him breathe
as he bowed to me. I thought to take his head
in my hands. To press my face to his cheeks,
but found his mouth opening wide. *You'll be
safer in here,* he told me. It was cold
and smelled of fish. I couldn't even see
my own hands, but heard the fighters fold
around us. *Took you long enough,* he sighed.
I am so old now, I've practically died.
I could tell my cat self was climbing through
walls, jumping from roof to roof. Inside
me, a light pulsed with each bump in the ride.
What is that? I cried. My body split in two.

My body split in two. I cried, *What is that?*
What started in my belly was in my lungs,
in my throat, in my eyes. I called to cat,
but there was no reply. Just my tongue
consumed by burning light. My eyes
caught fire and I was going blind. Then cat
spoke to me, but with my own voice this time.
We were speaking to ourselves. *Welcome back,*

we said. *Time to go.* And sight returned
at once, and this time, we could see the streets,
and everything upon them. Cat had given me
his eyes, and I'd risen to his mouth. Burned
a hole through his skull and climbed deep
in his thoughts. *It's hurting me!* He screamed.

He screamed, *It's hurting me!* In his thoughts,
which were also my own. And my body
wedged there like a sharp stone, wouldn't stop
drilling. The corpses of ghosts were dotting
the hills, but we were leaving them behind.
Somehow I knew to press harder, to join
my splitting forehead to the breach in cat's mind.
I was threadbare, made scarce, a dull coin
sinking in a fountain of breaking limbs.
Felt one side of me pass through cat, the other
stuck inside him. Everything fell quiet.
Soon he was no longer there. I felt him
drift away, fall apart. And another
something emerged. It was dark. It was light.

It was light. It was dark. Something emerged
from the mess of fur and flesh. I no longer
belonged to a body. Strings cut, I lurked
between muck and this glitch growing stronger
before me. Her body was twitching,
zeroes and ones slamming against her eyes.
She was tall and smelled of seaweed. Was pulling
the remnants of Cat and Kazumi's life
to her head. Smeared them across her brow,
linked their spines together like a crown.
The ground was shaking. Pixels vibrating.
Everything drowned in the glitch. The glitch drowned
in everything. I was flying up and down,
then, at last, I found I was me. And she,

at last, was me. I found then she and I
had grown controllers in our palms. I called
to cat, felt his pulse inside my arms. *Our time
is now*, we said at once. The glitch and all
her parts. Far away a heart was pumping
blood. Felt it pounding in our head—Master
stirring from sleep. We sprouted fins, a Gatling

gun from our back. Cat was exploding faster
in our bloodstream. Our fur returned. And ears
popped from the top of our head. We could hear
the echoes of the walls Master locked his heart
inside. We could hear the weapons he'd prepared.
He was already shooting. The danger was clear.
We became an I. I was ready to start.

We became an I. I was ready to start
my descent to the heart. It was buried
underground, beating hard, deep and dark.
I turned my fins to shovels, carried
a stick of dynamite inside my mouth.
But before I could begin to dig, Master
appeared before me. *But your heart is down*
within the earth! All his laser blasters
were aimed at my chest. *Yes*, he said, *I have*
no use for it anymore. He fired
and hit me in the lungs. I wasn't breathing.
I was seeing terrible things, a man
standing over me. He grabbed the wires
in my arms. I felt my heart exploding.

I felt my heart exploding. In my arms,
a note was ringing. It was screeching
through my body. It was becoming part
of me. Above it, Master was singing.
Your hands are gone, how will you live?
You cannot run, you cannot swim.
But I knew I still could move. I was glitch,
not bound by any rules. Beneath him,
I dove into the dirt. I was submarine,
and this was my sea. Master hadn't seen
me leave, so pleased was he with his deed.
I could hear his heart beating. It was screaming.
It knew I was there. It was scared. I leaned,
kissed it free. And Master crumbled into me.

In Master's mind, the start of me begun
with the ghosts to die. They asked me to drink,
to know the truth. They all touched me. At once,
I was trembling. In me, a dark sinking
hung about on the horizon. And more ghosts
circled me. Touched my head. One said, *hold on.*

He knew that I'd been waiting. Was I me?
I cried, *My body is split in two*. That what
he screamed was hurting me. In his thoughts
it was light. Something dark emerged. It was
me. And I found I was she. Then, at last,
I was ready. We became an I. To start,
in my arms, I felt my heart exploding.
Kissed it free. And Master crumbled into me.

Camp

At the funeral, I couldn't speak for her,
though I wanted to. Instead, I listened
to an uncle tell the story about the fishhook

she pulled from her hand, how it bled.
How she did not cry. When she tried
to tell me what it was like, I told her she

was lying. I didn't want to believe.
She took my head in her hand and cradled
me to her stomach. In that ear pressed

to her body, I knew the sound of the desert.
Wanted to descend into her past—I said
I'd take my hammer. I'd tear it down.

But when I got there, there was nothing
left to destroy, so I learned to destroy
myself. I thought she meant to live

with a fishhook in the palm of my hand.
I thought I was supposed to bleed
and never let my mother see me cry.

If she could see me now, this life,
this voice, I know she would say
I have been a fool. *Why do you try so hard*

to see my hands when you won't even look
at your own? Bachan, I am trying, but I still
open my palms without knowing what to hold.

Telephone Pole

Before the drawn emerged
into three dimensions,

power would have lived
in the trunk of it, the wires.

And the world would still
be flat, and nothing

would be named gravity.
The garland would be named

cure. Roses and jasmine,
the danger becoming knowable.

Sit with it, wait until it gives itself
away. A tremor of leaf,

stirring dust a distance away—
incrimination desires evidence.

To burn a witch, you must know
her name. To know her name,

show her she is invisible
as the river pulls her away.

This one is bobbing with apples
from orchards gone missing

at dawn. First there was a sign,
and a telephone pole,

and then they were gone.

Traume means Dream

The wires are crossed, so the explosion is inevitable.
Or not inevitable, evident. Like a mountain rigged
with trauma. Take a letter, drift into dream. Singed
cheeks, ears ringing—dive behind the barricade
for shelter. You'll never hear the way you did before,
but at least now you know death. It is the pitch that sinks
in your ear canals, that last gasping breath. Like
a telemarketer at dinner, ringing sinister
on the other side. But in this case, there is nothing
human. This is the trouble with drones, with walls
and firewalls. The soldier himself, behind him both
a government and no one.

If you are a soldier of trauma, you know what I mean.
There is an army inside the mountain. They are not
made of stone, but of dreams. The dreams are cracking,
not like eggs—like rocks, pounded to gravel inside
a prison. I don't want to make a metaphor of
suffering, but my wires are crossed as well. Want
to transform everything into gold, but my fingers
keep hissing and popping. Have to let what is heavy
drop to the floor. And love with my eyes alone,
my gloved hands pressed into a temple. This bead
is for your father. This bead is for your mother.
Even incense has a little bit of sulfur. Like a bomb,
or Old Faithful. Everywhere I go, it follows.

Séance For Michael Brown

Let the bullets rise like sparrows
chirping from your chest, back
to the nests from which they flew,
let them pull back to the spool of life
your strings, renewed and uncut,
let every breath return to you. Let
the sirens sleep an eternal slumber,
let us steal a boat and leave this island,
row out to the shore of a house built
on the foundation of every language
that's ever been taken from us. Weave
bricks with our tongues, sculpt our walls
until they become impenetrable, summon
our ancestors and party like it's 1492,
so nobody will be able to say a thing
about it. I wish poetry could do this,
want to stack my words, one upon
another, grab your hands through
the clouds and climb back down
with you, wish poetry could slip
into that strand of time that runs
alongside mine, tell you this time
when you return, this time it'll be
different. Wish the poem could wrap
its loving arms around you, bring you
back into the circle of those I've found
here on earth, wish poems could fill you
with life the way it fills those alive, wish
there were something I could say worth
saying, but you're gone. What do I do
with these words, dragging themselves
away from my useless tongue, what do
I do to resuscitate you? I keep clinging
to the hope that I can heal us, but all
I do is heal myself, find in my poems
a way to pull from my own body
the pebbles of something buried inside
me, and it is not the same—so let this
be the poem that changes me,

let me burn every oppressive word
I've ever spoken, cull from my bones
all the poison I've been given.
I will never stop speaking your name.

Bruce Lee's Fist Is Cut Open by a Glass Bottle

We begin with the bone as it culls
a river to mouth, then zoom out,
and everything grows

into something else. Soon Bruce,
too, will zoom beyond
the green of Hollywood screens

to take his place among the stars,
his body laid to rest beside
Nisei stolen in a war to be seen

as something other
than body. And what can be said
about that? It is 1973, my mother

still hears people scream *Jap*
as she walks down the street,
and my grandmother's name

will never be her own. But this
is not the story I meant to tell—
look at Bruce's bones,

giving to the flames in them
their marrow, like the hearts
of mangoes taking on fire

in the rubble of Chinatown
as it burns. This cremation,
this incineration, and no,

there is no phoenix incubation
there, nothing to rise
from ashes. The year is 1906,

then—San Francisco, not
reborn. And Bruce is still
the name of a future unclaimed,

a desire before the body
that fails it. His knuckle not yet
gashed passage, not open well,

not yet ready to stare him down,
no depth of death lodged
like a grain of rice in his skin.

And everyone hasn't decided
they want to be like Bruce Lee.
And we, with the face

of Bruce have not yet been reduced
to lean, mean, fighting Chinese.
No, this is the before—

we're still here, lingering inside
a burning city, sweating fumes
like a swelling body, blood rushing

to skin to lick the tip of that glass
mosquito, and in this body
there is nobody left

to shout. Because Bruce knows
his skin cannot help but kiss
the fists of men who despise him,

cannot help but burn crop circles
into its own grasses, cannot help
the way that just beneath

the surface, the Bruce's bruises
are collecting like pools of fire,
rising, right there, and simmering.

Karma Speaks Back

No, I'm not a bitch. Face it—
I'm more starling than dog. More
speckled with night, more god-light

strung in every color across your sky.
I pray in a tongue more beautiful
than yours, fly back in the faces

of those who confuse their own gaze,
their own wide eyes, skin ruptured
by teeth twice spoken. Borrow me,

make me your apple, flesh of night,
black soot on winding wing,
pluck me from a cloud, the stuffed

pillow of a dream you fall into
without seeing. Empty that chorus
of dog-song in my blood and name it

me. I'll be mongrel, you be king.
Put a dress on me, call me the last
of the castrati. If only you could be

less twinkling eye, less nitrogen sky.
If only you could see how alone
you are, star of your own unmaking.

Becoming Mermaid

Never with such force have I touched
anyone. Never so firm against any
page. With each print that is made,
the light emerges in tiny candles.
From a distance, they disappear.

To be clear, I thought I could go away
like this. Flip a switch, silence
the sonogram. Back before

emergence, swelling. The wonder in me
was dying. I was birthing my own
aborting, erupting with the remnants
of myself, charcoal on my face, coal dripping
down the wells in my skin, the river
in my veins stagnating. I thought

I'd missed out. My hair wouldn't grow.
My body held in no one's hands.

I was a sheet on a clothesline, white sun,
only skin. I could see myself, the stars
opening in me. My hair slicked back

like my father's. I was nothing
but a second printing, pale light
pushing through my belly—

Until I kissed the page, full of holes.
My lips turned to wings, turned the sky
to pulpy leaves. I could see anything
if I took my mouth from it. So I took
my mouth from me. And kissed
this mess untended.

Narcissus Explains

I say I am drawn to masked dances,
but the dance is only a distraction. Make me
a faceless man. Let me lose his likeness.
Lose this ghost I sing to in the shower,

let his face be not mine. I tire of it,
want to lose the cliff of my chin
to the waves that beat against it,
but I am sculpted like him,

I am ice in deep winter, no hibernation,
cold and calculated, glass burning like a moth
to the grave I consecrated—let me be
my own maker, baker of goods I keep

inside the sheets of my own body;
I will bake me a cake as fast
as I can, let it rise in my eyes
and reshape them, I am no snowman—

Let my jawline be slim and beautiful,
I want nothing but to unroll myself, to know
the knife, again and again, give me a father
to ignore me, teach me to sin, give me

something else to know myself by—I watch
myself smile, I watch myself cry. It is not
enough to say I am here. I keep looking
for the girl, but she always disappears.

'I only' is not the I of 'is,' but 'at'

Tonight I stay home with a girl,
a hip poet. And I don't know how
her books dance. And I want to know,
to move up in a footwork

I lost with her, learn music,
pretending my back, my skin slipped
into boxes, is not a skirt of air
finished with invisibility fabric,

already heavy from me. I find something
here, syncing until it hurts,
graciously. She and I sneak beyond
our bodies somewhere—smiles, slow dance,

the hand on my back a few Christmases ago,
last there a second New Year's. I'm out
to be invited into forgiveness.
But none do as she's now.

The girl and I thought reading books,
and working more, and sleeping in,
doing college, busy librarian, to eventually...
For months I spent my degree

sharing sleep in a finished poem
about my divorcee parents,
or the 'real' son. I'm guilty, don't
know when I'm finally done.

And then this just stops. I was not
packing much but my Louis CK into
tomorrow, no summer. I was feeling
what's in the harm

of it, didn't dance a night, breathed
an apartment hall awake with what
resurfaces, rapidly leading back out
of our last August boxes.

We begin on a summer whim to pack up
and go to Sacramento. I had another
chance, making now the future, ready
to go back. But to think, finally, is to know

I'm not done. And I've done a second
dance lesson. And when 'up' is motion itself,
it's up to her, watching me. As in, I wasn't
dreamed until now.

With Lines From Stephanie, Kelly, Matt, Cam & Kim

If today were a poem, I'd make it a sonnet.
In the poem, my father would be perfectly willing
to hold my many stitched parts, and my sister
would be end-stopped somewhere

with light-up dials because this would be
the landscape of women I've loved, cut too short.
This would be a different poem if I wanted to say
what matters are napkins, but I don't, of course,

because of a man, white flowers in a vase, the volta
on my back, ached with wonder. And in the space
the poem leaves me, O sleeping bees, let me finish

what I started, kiss my hands all the way down
the page. It's true I can never go home, but I have
these words among the world, awake, & speechless.

To the dead bees on the windowsill
and also my friends—

I'm sorry I said those things.
I was wrong. Poetry
doesn't do anything, not really.
There's a man out there, and he's

killing himself, or he's
killing someone else,
and the poem's not going
to stop him.

There's a dead man who can't be
undead, not even
in the poem. And don't get me started
on the wars.

So we'll just leave him there. With all the flowers,
the fields full of bees, dying off
by the thousands. And everything dies,

I know that. We walk outside and see the clouds,
and the red-tail hawk
that hunts from the tree
across the bus stop. It's killing
something, every day killing

a father, a mother, a child.
It's not the same, I know,
and the poem's not going to stop
him, either.
But sometimes I think it can.

Like when a dead person emerges in the poem and speaks.
It's the ultimate projection,
we can't ever know

what the dead want.
And they can't be

anything but the reflection

of a face
in a rushing river, broken up,

hardly even there. And the reflection
never gets swept away, really, which
is a problem—but also a solution,

because then all your dead bees
can mean something
different. The dead

are dead, yes, but I'm alive,
and my friends are alive,

and I want that to be beautiful.
I can't even look at myself

without wanting a river to cut up my face
and carry me somewhere else.
But I see you, bees, and I think

I killed you. Give me your burdens,
and I'll put them in the poem, ask
the poem to carry them. No problem.

It can hold a lot, it's quite sturdy.
If you throw it in the river
it'll still be in my head.

If you take my head
off, it'll still be in the river.
And when

the river is my head, and the poem is
my river, and the head of the poem is

for bees, and the foot of the poem
returns to bees, then I feel strangely
complete.

No. There are no
fathers in this poem.
And let's say there are no men

and they are not dying, because I'm sorry,
I meant to take them out, and give you this instead.

Which is why I did this, anyway, bees,
in the first place, for you.

Not Christmas Time

The world is awash in beauty. For so long
I've wanted to write this, and today
I don't care anymore what anyone thinks,

so here it is. Car windows catching snow,
nose hairs that freeze with each breath—
I am alive! I could break
my windows or
trim my nose hairs! I could lie
face down in the snow and sing jingle bells!

It's past Christmas time, yes.
But if you were a Californian dreaming
of white Christmases for twenty-three years,
you'd frolic gaily, too.

Last night, I drew these little butterflies
or snowflakes, tossed them aside.
Even now, I can't tell what it is that flew
from my hands. Let's say they're snowflakes.

Better yet,
let's tear them apart! I can do whatever,
because I can.

I like snow, but sometimes
I want to obliterate it all, or just go back home—
take all these suitcases and head west
in our station wagon. I know

the world's not awash in beauty.
I just wanted to say that. It's this kitchen,
this living room full of suitcases, this basement
caked in mud. When I rip butterflies

to shreds it is because
I write too many poems
where nothing breaks and nothing dies. Poems lying
on a small beautiful bed, staring at the sky,

buried under so much weight and all that.
This is not that poem. Actually it is.

But I would write about butterflies
a hundred times if you told me to.

I would bury myself in the snow
and stuff my face with it,
kiss it until my lips turned blue—

There's this girl, sitting across from me,
taking pictures of me on her Instagram.
I would stay here and write about

all these things that don't matter,
if you always show me your Instagram and also
your poems.

See, the world is really just awash
in you, only it's not the world,

it's me, and I'm not even here, really,
just words emerging from cocoon,
which means that all of this is you.

Sumi

for my grandmother

She would name the sun as it rose
the moon, so that when the moon
was setting, the moon would also
rise. She would name the river
the ocean, and watch as it flowed
endlessly into itself. She would name
the rain, the clouds. The light, the dark.
The desert she would name the coast.
One day, she would return there
to name me.
                    Kazu for peace,
Mi for beauty, so that I would become
both of these, just as she. Su, for endless,
Mi, as in me, we, the river, the ocean,
endless. And she, the beauty
inside me.

Sonnet Ending with Love

The biggest change happened when I stopped
carrying my thoughts in that handbag. I dropped
them off on the train and watched them drift
into the sun. I was drawn to endings, to missed
connections, then—to carousels and ocean waves
rising and swelling. The wagon circles had paved
the way for me to follow. So I never sent
for anyone, but you gave me your letter to bend
around my body, self-addressed, signed, sealed,
no postage needed, like the words were enough.
As if these wrists wrapped with scars were tough
and I could write my name over anything. Real
life was a bird, on fire. It burned me, stuffed
me in its breast. I wrote it down, called it love.

The Very Last New Year's Resolution

The very last mammoth was just like the others,
except more lonely. The very last tortilla chip
makes me feel guilty. The very last line
of the poem changes everything about
what came before. On the very last day
of any semester, if I liked my class, I buy them
cookies. Every year, someone hears the very last
words of any given language, and then
it sinks into the mud of colonialism. White
soldiers gave every last Indian at Fort Pitt
a blanket, to keep them warm. The very last
samurai was white. The very last thing
I wanted this poem to be about was white
people. But that didn't last too long. Last
year, I wavered between whispering
and screaming. The very latest from
the western front: a lasting quiet. The radio
was never much of a conversationalist.
The very last tape I ever listened to
scrambled like an egg at brunch
in Pittsburgh on a Sunday, with
the very last people I'd ever expected
to be at brunch with. Who knew I'd love
so many white people. The very last story
my grandmother told me was about a boy
named Tsutomo. He was born from a peach
called America. The very last place his father
thought he'd ever be. The very last ornament
we hang from our tree each year is a face.
The very last year I spent Christmas with
my whole family was in 6th grade. I hated
my whole family that year. To the very last
drop of blood in my body, I wanted them
out. Now I want to bring all these Pittsburgh
people home with me. Take them to meet
my family. With every pixel of every word
I bleed. I never wanted to hate my family.
Or anything at all. I want last year to be
the very last time that I ever hate anything.
Even when white people are killing black

people and sealing off the street. I will hold
so many hands. To the very last finger
resting on every last trigger of every
last gun. Listen to me, I am loving, I am loving,
I am giving so much fucking love to you.

Occupation

You got to be kitten me right meow, said the not-funny coach to mammoth, who was not amused. *Language escapes me,* he spat back. *You mistake me for a human.*

That space journey cat took with the coach had turned cat into a mammoth, though it never really felt right in cat's head. *Meow,* the mammoth would hum in his head. *Meow, meow, meow.*

But the Japanese were ripping the coach's playbook to shreds. And were teaching mammoth to mew. *Like a proper Japanese kitten,* they said.

To be kitten, apply one strip of wallpaper at a time. Purr and frolic in the floral print. *Language cannot grow when we don't teach it the ways of civilization,* the Japanese star said.

So mammoth used language. He loved the idea of farms and cities. You got me, he said to coach, as the star held the remains of cat's bloody body in its mouth. *Right,* said coach.

Meow, mammoth said, before realizing his mistake. He tried to repent for his sins. *Mew, mew, mew.* But the soldiers had already heard. They shot him and turned him into a piano.

You mistake me for a piano, the piano said. *You got to be kitten me. Right,* the star said. *You got me. Meow.* And the piano sang a sad song about a fish who lost his head and grew a human female.

Becoming Mermaid

This body bears no resemblance to the bodies
of the past. This body is only here, as it is,
right now, and so this history
of other bodies does not concern it.

There has never been another swimmer
inside the body, not as this body swims,
not as this one.

But when I move an arm, there is another arm moving.
And inside that arm, another, and so on. This is how
I understand it. Child, you,

immigrant not yet arrived.
You will see the shore and wonder why it is
that you came. You will be offered six seeds

and no acre of land. And the seeds will not be
what they say they are. They bloom only
in winter, and only in your hands.

Sometimes at night the eels sneak inside me
and they find her, the child,
and I emerge from my dreams

of a past life. I was a girl who loved
to dress up for parties. She was left-handed,
and did not belong to them. She painted her nails
every day and her favorite color was purple.

She came from a town not far off the coast.
She was not beautiful. She looked like me.

If it appears to you as the sun, it is most likely the sun.
If it appears as rain, it is most likely rain.

I wanted it all. I have burned countless dresses
and set them on clotheslines to hang,
but each time they float away.

To cross a border with a dress. To cross-dress.
Who died on a cross, who lived by the cross,
who crossed their heart and hoped to die,
I am crossing the street to you now,

tell me you will take me,
tell me you will take me home.

A History of Fire

Before the sea opened
its mouth, I was swallow,

black, wax-slicked feathers,
air clinging like oil—couldn't preen

that lack out of me. Kept myself dry,

high above the crest
of the tide. All this time, touching

nothing. Footprint
in the snow, a reflection disturbed,

only my mouth, wet, breath
stuck chiming in my lungs.

This is a history of breathlessness
squeezed from tongues, of tiny words

untied from chests.

Where do I fit
beyond the wonder of these bones?

In this history I have flown
empty as a bowl.

Before my wings, there was sun.
Before the sun, I renounced my name.

Before the name, I was match
and flame, before being pulled apart.

Happy Together

At Iguazu, the water pounding
the air to a pulp,
under that pressure, screaming
from the cold.

(To lose a house, learn Portuguese. Fall in love
with the swaying of your tongue,
the fullness of a kite, hold all that wind—
turn, and let it go.)

And you look at me
like I am the secret you hide
in your sleeve—and you say,
I loved you. Back there,
in the falls.

(And how translation befuddles
the most astute cameras, whose only means
is darkness. And how the falls
are plural, but this one. The waterfall,
falling water, fall of each breath, still
filling the fall air.)

   Though now, who's to say?
Love hits like
a fly across your lip, so believe
that it was never there—
but feel the beat
of tender wings.

And fill poems with
what could be angels. And the words
against a landscape of red dirt and rainbows,
planting seeds of something
we can't identify in the soil.

(The branches of the trees cling
to each other, drops of water,
everything falling, then, and the rain on the stage.

I keep writing this
story to tell another.)

Matter harvested
from cast off pages,
my skull cracking open before me.
A window into you, back there,
but closed now.

(Master, you'd mastered
the art of me, stuck me inside your sleeve,
took me out, when I loved you.)

And I touched the glass to find
it shattering, saw
behind me the river wanting
a feast, drinking me
until I'd lost my very last key,
and the cities fell beneath me.

When will I find what swims
from my hands? What lock
has left this hole in me?

I was a goldfish, pulled
from the sun.
You put me back
in the pond. And I was running
from you, and the falls,
a heap of sinking bones. And
I was hidden, too,
        when I lost you.

Collateral

The wind itself makes no sound,
but we give to it a howling.
Take away the possibility

of forward, and the subject
will change directions.
The bonsai knows this,

its stunted limbs turned
horizontal—though it does
not howl. We admire the patient

in its complicity. To dedicate
one's life toward becoming
beautiful. How patient, also,

the hands tending this one foot
tree with such precision. Binding
branches against wind. To appear

so wild. But wild it is not.
And the wind can never stop
howling. And howling

is not the fence that cuts
through the night. It is the sun,
a thousand breaths falling.

Gyoza

I know when I return home
at last, my mother will take a knife
to cabbage for hours, will fold
dumpling skins and drop them

into boiling water, will stop
to pull back with cracked fingers
her hair, now white. It will catch
the light and glow. And I will want it

black. When I close my eyes I can see
her dark, dark hair. I am guilty of burning
her body this way. The fire erupts
from within me. I am obsessed

to the point of hunger, each limb
engulfed by flame. When I was five,
I believed I could become a mother.
I could sink inside my wrists so slim.

I could sometimes starve myself, too.
When I looked in the mirror,
there were tiny bows in my hair. Pink.
Yes, I have wanted to be glamorous.

I have wanted ribbons, the girl
in the mirror. Her smile could hit those notes
I could not. If I could touch her I would.
But I would not give my body to another.

There is nothing romantic about this.
To ask her to become beautiful
I had to forget that my mother
is my mother. I wanted her to look

the way she did at 30—No, I can't seem
to speak truthfully. I wanted her to be
in love. I thought it could make her rise
like oil to the surface of her body. Please,

I take it back. Her hair, her hands, her knife.
I would ask that this be beautiful. Would ask
that this be love. Would ask that she be oil,
that she be water, for her always to rise like that.

Rachel This One Is For You

Did you wear your cat ears today?
Life is too short to not wear cat ears

And sit on the hood of your car
and eat the peanut butter straight from the jar

We've never done this together
but it seems like something we might do
if there were birds involved

or cats or Ariana Grande
or capitalist power structures
or Amazon Prime

I say Amazon Prime because whenever I use my sister's account
I think of you and how upset you must be
With me

For being such a terrible socialist

But how you'll forgive me

Because we can't climb out of Schrodinger's box
when we live inside it

And how you'll say it's okay
to like Amazon Prime
and cats
and Ariana

Even when the box pulls histories inside it
And spits them out in the street to bleed
What is there to do but work and write

And sometimes watch Gilmore Girls
So many episodes of Gilmore Girls

that I don't know
if I'm alive or dead

Am I even real anymore
I think

And Alexis Bledel is actually Mexican
except she's white most of the time

And I start thinking *I'm* white
Because the box *won't* kill *me*

There is no paradox
When *I'm* there

But there is

Because in Missoula
a man asked me where I was hiding my AKs

and if I was invading

And I was
And I am

I love Ariana but she's still white

And I love you too

I am wearing my cat ears

POWER

for Adrienne Rich

What I have found here, shining. I chased
the sun across the same desert that cars
in commercials are always crossing,
that desert somewhere that stands
for all deserts, for Nissan and for Ford.

I see it, when I say desert. There are cliffs
in the distance, too. Maybe Eastwood was here,
with some feathered caricatures staring
down at him. I'm so done with everyone.

Today I spoke,
and someone's ego was punctured. Too bad,
he deserved it. I have coins in my purse,
and they clang around. Sometimes I spend
them. Words are like this. Except each
is a mirror. And we're hurtling across a room
full of them, every day.

It's hard to ignore
the ones that hit you in the face.
Easy to ignore the rest.
But look closer.

Everything I write condemns me. There is
no such thing as an accident. I write about
deserts because I am drawn to death. I am
thinking about cars because of
that oil change I need,

and how pitiful it is that I can't do it
myself. I can fix a computer, I can revise
a poem, I can rescue dying plants
from going under. See, there's me
and my obsession with death again.

So what died in the desert? If you know
me, you know. Touch my face, read my name.
I am so predictable. Here's another desert image:
an oil well, the slow, mechanical grind.

There are thousands of these behind
my sister's apartment.

She uses words
in the classroom, modeling how to sharpen
a pencil correctly. You get up, making
as little noise as possible. You walk, not run,
to the pencil sharpener, where you slowly
put the pencil in, gently,
and apply a very small amount of force.
If it doesn't work, instead of getting
frustrated and slamming the pencil
against the desk, you should call
on the teacher, and ask her to help.

This is the way
you write a poem. Only there is
no teacher, there is only you, with your
words, betraying you. Everyone
is laughing at you, there is pig blood
hanging from your hair.

Your body
is laid bare. And everything beneath it.

I want to fix it all. Again, and again.
Because the hands at my neck
are my own. They are mine,
and mine alone. Adrienne—
You have given me this.

Everything I write
condemns me.

Becoming Kazumi

There's a phone ringing in the back of my mind
that I refuse to pick up. And I swallowed the receiver
years ago, anyway, during one of those fits
where I throw my whole life into the dryer
and come out static and

I'm balling up my clothes again,
it always feels like laundry time, and I'm just writing
a stupid poem that doesn't say anything.

The gloves on the table are not mine. The words
that spear my tongue somehow bubble out of me
without my having done anything.

I want to live inside someone else's poems
but I only have my own. And in mine, my father never

appears, but today he texted me about the -8 degree
weather, because he loves me. That's the thing,
we always say stuff in the stupidest of ways.
Here I am, singing like Ariana

even though I'll never be. There is no one to be
but myself, worrying that I'm this genie
in a bottle made of diamonds that even diamonds

can't cut through.
I'm not a mermaid. I'm not a pop star. I'm a little kid
swimming in the body of a man. This is the poem that's supposed
to get me out of this mess. But I just keep diving in.

So let me love the diving. Let me never know.
I, too, can wear my own crown.

I, too, can part the waves and call them sand.
And I'll sit on this imaginary beach which is also
an ocean. And I'll be a fish, singing,
because why the fuck not. And everything
will swirl around me like a giant cocoon

and I'll be here, chilling, looking everyone in the eye
as I'm treading water, or sand, or schools of little silver fish,
or giant puddles of jelly, I'll just stare everyone down, super hard,

and be like, *what.*

Gratitude

Thank you to those who have helped to make this book a possibility. My teachers Yona, Lynn, Terrance, Dawn, & Toi: more than anything, you've given me your way of observing and knowing and listening, and so of course, too, poetry.

Thank you Pittsburgh poets. Thank you Malcolm, for loving best my most ridiculous poems I didn't think were worth holding on to. Thank you Caleb, for helping me to find the parts of me I'd lost. Thank you Stephanie, for knowing what it was I was trying to do when I didn't even know it myself.

Thank you ancestors, thank you family, thank you mom, dad, Sami.

Thank you Michelle; look at us, in this House of Godzilla. I used to think we'd be on top of the world, but I know now we're building a better one together. This book is a collaborative effort; I am a collaborative effort. I carry with me all of your love; and this record of all I have found with you. At one time I was, you were, we were, and now continue to be, in this form, a having happened.

<3 <3 <3.

Acknowledgments

Telephone Pole & Collateral in *Twelfth House*

The Last New Year's Resolution in Split This Rock's Poetry Database

Camp in *HEArt*

Becoming Ariana & The Obsession Is Real in *glitterMOB*

Occupation in *Wu-Wei Fashion Mag*

Becoming Mermaid in *Rogue Agent*

Bruce Lee's Fist Is Cut Open by a Glass Bottle in *Boxcar Poetry Review*

Kazumi as Sailor Moon in *Ilanot Review*

Homeland Security Arrests Godzilla Without Reading Him His Miranda Rights as White Christmas Fills the Air & Pyongyang Poem in *Barrelhouse Magazine*

About the Poet

Kazumi Chin is a poet from California, where he works to build loving communities with marginalized people, to put language to the mechanisms of structures and identities, and to create spaces and tools that allow others to do the same. He is interested in scholarship at the intersection of art-making and critical theory, and has a profound love for maps, spreadsheets, algorithms, taxonomies, simulations, and also poetry & the mythical power of true friendship.

About the Press

Sibling Rivalry Press is an independent press based in Little Rock, Arkansas. It is a sponsored project of Fractured Atlas, a nonprofit arts service organization. Contributions to support the operations of Sibling Rivalry Press are tax-deductible to the extent permitted by law, and your donations will directly assist in the publication of work that disturbs and enraptures. To contribute to the publication of more books like this one, please visit our website and click *donate*.

Sibling Rivalry Press acknowledges the following donors, without whom this book would not be possible:

TJ Acena	JP Howard	Tina Parker
Kaveh Akbar	Shane Khosropour	Brody Parrish Craig
John-Michael Albert	Randy Kitchens	Patrick Pink
Kazim Ali	Jørgen Lien	Dennis Rhodes
Seth Eli Barlow	Stein Ove Lien	Paul Romero
Virginia Bell	Sandy Longhorn	Robert Siek
Ellie Black	Ed Madden	Scott Siler
Laure-Anne Bosselaar	Jessica Manack	Alana Smoot Samuelson
Dustin Brookshire	Sam & Mark Manivong	Loria Taylor
Alessandro Brusa	Thomas March	Hugh Tipping
Jessie Carty	Telly McGaha & Justin Brown	Alex J. Tunney
Philip F. Clark	Donnelle McGee	Ray Warman & Dan Kiser
Morell E. Mullins	David Meischen	Ben Westlie
Jonathan Forrest	Ron Mohring	Valerie Wetlaufer
Hal Gonzlaes	Laura Mullen	Nicholas Wong
Diane Greene	Eric Nguyen	Anonymous (18)
Brock Guthrie	David A. Nilsen	
Chris Herrmann	Joseph Osmundson	

CPSIA information can be obtained
at www.ICGtesting.com
Printed in the USA
FSHW021316081019
62812FS